Decorating
pumpkins
& gourds

Decorating pumpkins & gourds

20 fun & stylish projects for decorating pumpkins, gourds, and squashes

Deborah Schneebeli-Morrell

CICO BOOKS

LONDON NEW YORK

For Raphael, Suraya, and Luna

This edition published in 2018 by CICO Books
an imprint of Ryland Peters & Small
20-21 Jockey's Fields, London, WC1R 4BW
341 E 116th St., New York, NY 10029

www.rylandpeters.com

10 9 8 7 6 5 4 3 2 1

First published in 2008 by CICO Books

A CIP catalog record for this book is available from the Library of Congress and
the British Library.

ISBN-13: 978 1 78249 601 4

Printed in China

Editor: Gillian Haslam
Designer: Christine Wood
Photographer: Heini Schneebeli
Stylist: Deborah Schneebeli-Morrell
Illustrator: Trina Dalziel

contents

introduction

Pumpkins, gourds and squash all belong to the *Cucurbitaceae* family, which is one of the largest groups of vegetables. They have the most descriptive and intriguing names, from the huge segmented Rouge Vif d'Etampes to the tiny, dark green rolets or the beautiful chrome yellow sweet dumpling. The smooth, speckled skin of the fig leaf gourd is so different to the ivory white of the cotton candy pumpkin, only the shape convincing us they are from the same family.

Their stunning and brilliant tones, patterns and colours are redolent of the fruitfulness of autumn, and their curious assortment of shapes makes them adaptable not only for the garden and table but for decoration, and in particular for adaptation into beautiful and original lanterns.

Many of these vegetables have intriguing common names, inspired by their colouring or shape. In the projects that follow, I have named the varieties I have used. However, the availability of varieties does vary tremendously according to location and time of year. With this in mind, many of the projects can easily be adapted, allowing you to use whatever varieties you are able to buy or grow.

Gather your pumpkins, squash and gourds together in a vibrant display and live with them for a while before you become inspired to begin decorating them.

pumpkins, squash and gourds

Pumpkins are the most common member of the large cucurbit family. As a rule, they tend to be large (some reach huge proportions, such as the Atlantic Giant, and inspire avid competition amongst their growers), and their flesh and skin are softer. This makes them the easiest to scoop out and to create a cut-through decoration; however, the watery flesh is therefore less flavoursome when cooked. The most famous are the well-known field or Halloween pumpkins (see page 86). These are grown in their millions and are the most frequently seen pumpkins in supermarkets, being sold for making spooky lanterns at Halloween.

A squash is really a firmer-fleshed and longer-lasting type of pumpkin. They are cured in the sun after harvest to harden the skin and will consequently last for months. The flesh can be really dense but equally delicious, often having a rich, chestnutty flavour, and these are the best for soups, pies and baking. It is one of the most highly prized vegetables with the advantage that the seeds are equally nutritious.

Gourds were the first vessels – long before the invention of pottery, early peoples fashioned them into bottles, culinary utensils, musical instruments and toys. They are still used in some cultures around the world and, because they have a tough skin

when dried, they lend themselves to intricate forms of design. Some notable examples from Africa are very valuable and can be found in ethnographic collections in the best museums. It is widely thought that the ubiquitous gourd was distributed around the world by floating on the currents of the great oceans.

growing your own

If you are able to, it is a good idea to grow a collection of different pumpkins (the varieties available and even the names will vary according to where you live). The gourd family produces its fascinating and colourful fruit on vigorous vines which can look stunning when grown up obelisks or along pergolas in a decorative vegetable garden.

Pumpkins and squash are easy to grow but need lots of space. Sow the seeds in pots in spring and plant out in a rich soil when all risk of frost has passed. Pinch out the tips of the trailing shoots to encourage fruit formation. Feed occasionally and harvest your delicious crop in the autumn after the leaves have died down, leaving the brilliantly coloured fruit to decorate the bare earth.

It is best to buy in fresh seed as the collected seed doesn't always come true. Bees love the huge yellow flowers and have a wonderful way of cross-fertilizing the well-known varieties. The easiest and most rewarding squash to grow are crown prince, butternut, kabocha and sweet dumpling.

carving techniques

Most of the projects in this book can be created using everyday tools that you might find in your home toolbox or you can use kitchen cutlery. You can divide the tools into those used for preparing the squash, gourd or pumpkin, and those used for the decoration.

preparation

Since most of the pumpkins or squash are used as lanterns and are lit from inside, you need to begin by removing the 'lid' – the top (or sometimes the base) of the pumpkin. This usually means cutting a circular hole, allowing for the seeds and flesh to be removed, and reducing the thickness of the wall (a thinner wall makes it easier to carve or pierce the decoration).

The firmness of the flesh will vary from squash to pumpkin to gourd, and you will find that you will need to use an assortment of knives, spoons and scoops to help you remove the flesh. For the varieties with the hardest flesh, a flat-ended woodcarving tool can be used to prize away the flesh. You may also need to shred the flesh with the point of a kitchen knife before removing it with a spoon or scoop. You will need to be careful and patient, so it is best to start with a project that uses a softer fleshed variety.

decoration

The decoration of pumpkins, squash and gourds usually takes the form of cutting away pieces of the thinned wall in order to allow the light to shine through. This can be done with a sharp, pointed knife, a special pumpkin saw for the tougher skinned varieties, or a gimlet which is a small tool used to make neat, round holes.

Another rather magical form of decoration is created by using a lino-cutting tool. This has a V-shaped blade which engraves a narrow line on the skin of the pumpkin without cutting through. As the wall of the pumpkin has been made thinner, you will find that the light will penetrate these engraved lines, adding another layer of decoration.

The lanterns are lit with short good-quality, slow-burning candles or nightlights that stand in a glass jar within the pumpkin. As dusk darkens into night, the pumpkin lanterns will glow brighter. You can also insert outdoor fairy lights to create a sparkling glow.

tools

A small flat-ended woodcarving tool is useful when cutting away very hard flesh.

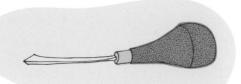

You will need a craft knife or two, perhaps one with a more pointed blade. A sharp, pointed, small kitchen knife is also essential.

A special pumpkin saw is useful for the hard-skinned varieties. It has the advantage of being safer than a kitchen knife if it slips.

For scooping out the flesh and seeds you will need an assortment of spoons in different sizes. You can also make your own special tool by bending over the handle of a dessertspoon so it fits into the pumpkin easily. A special pumpkin scoop is very useful when reducing the thickness of the wall.

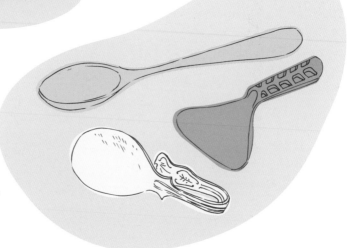

A nylon pot scourer is useful for smoothing the inside.

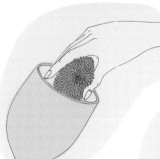

A water-soluble crayon is helpful for drawing your design directly on the skin of the pumpkin. This can be wiped off with a damp cloth. For other projects, a ballpoint pen makes a neat line and the ink can be cut away with your design.

Piercing tools are useful, such as a bradawl for marking designs and a couple of gimlets in different sizes for making neat holes.

A lino-cutting tool is one of the most useful tools and it will enable you to make sophisticated and stylish decoration. This is readily available from a good art supplier.

If you really enjoy carving pumpkins, assemble a small group of favoured tools which you can keep in a special bag to bring out each year when the squash and pumpkin season begins once more.

the projects

birds in a bush

In this pretty project, a number of small field pumpkins have been engraved with charming images of birds. The pumpkins are small enough to wedge into the tangled branches of the thorn bush and, when lit, the birds glow a deep, vibrant yellow against the orange outer skin of the fruit.

Look for images of birds in books and magazines – you only need a few lines to indicate feathers, a wing or a tail. You may get carried away and create a whole flock of birds to make a stunning original outdoor decoration.

you will need

- 3 small field pumpkins
- water-soluble crayon
- craft knife
- small kitchen knife
- assorted small scooping spoons (a long-handled teaspoon is useful)
- nylon pot scourer
- paper and pen, for making a template
- dressmaker's pins
- bradawl
- lino-cutting tool
- nightlights and glass jars

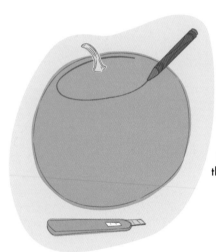

1 Using the crayon, draw a circle around the stem at the top of the pumpkin – this needs to be sizeable enough to allow you to manipulate the tools inside, but doesn't need to be large enough to insert your hand. Cut out with the craft knife, and, if necessary, use a kitchen knife to release the 'lid' before removal.

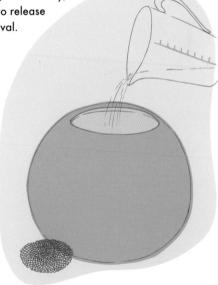

2 Scoop out the flesh and seeds and reduce the thickness of the shell to about 8mm (⅜in). It is important to make sure the inner base is flat as this is where the jar will stand. Rub the inside with the pot scourer to create a smooth surface and rinse with water to remove all the debris.

3 Draw a bird outline onto a piece of paper, making the bird a size that fits neatly onto the surface of your chosen pumpkin. As the surface will be curved, make sure that you leave enough space above and below the motif so that all of the image will be visible without distortion.

4 Pin the template onto the surface of the pumpkin and prick out the bird motif with the bradawl.

tip
Although instructions are given for using a template, it is always better to draw the image directly onto the surface of the pumpkin. You will need some skill and confidence to do this but this comes quickly with practice. The advantage of using a water-soluble crayon means that you can rub away any lines until you are happy with the result.

5 Remove the template and use the lino-cutting tool to create the outline of the bird, following the guidelines made with the bradawl. Indicate the tail and wing with two and three lines respectively. Engrave a simple arc for the breast and nick out a few dots as decoration inside the breast line. Add the eye and beak.

6 Engrave a couple of lines to represent the ground and create the flowers and leaves on either side of the bird. Place the nightlight in a small glass jar and insert into the pumpkin before lighting.

LEFT AND BELOW: *Create a whole flock of birds with different markings and plumage to decorate your garden at dusk.*

bengali gourds

Pumpkins, gourds and squash are common vegetables in the diets of many differing cultures, with some varieties grown in the Asian subcontinent seldom seen in the West. Due to the movement of peoples around the globe, in many of our cities we can now find wonderful shops that sell exotic and intriguing ingredients for these immigrant populations.

These lovely smooth-skinned gourds are highly favoured in Bangladeshi cuisine. The soft skin and white flesh make them easy to scoop out and carve, whilst the cool green colour and variety of elegant shapes make a welcome contrast to the fiery reds and oranges of the more traditional pumpkins.

you will need

● 3 green bengali gourds in assorted colours and shapes
● craft knife
● kitchen knife
● assorted scooping spoons
● flat-edged woodcarving tool
● nylon pot scourer
● lino-cutting tool
● small gimlet
● large gimlet
● string of outdoor fairy lights

1 Cut a circle into the base of the gourd using the craft knife, using the kitchen knife to release it if necessary. This hole will need to be large enough for you to insert your hand when holding the scooping spoon.

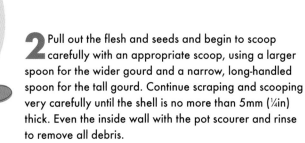

2 Pull out the flesh and seeds and begin to scoop carefully with an appropriate scoop, using a larger spoon for the wider gourd and a narrow, long-handled spoon for the tall gourd. Continue scraping and scooping very carefully until the shell is no more than 5mm (¼in) thick. Even the inside wall with the pot scourer and rinse to remove all debris.

3 To decorate the long gourd, make a series of slits lengthwise around the shell. To decorate the round gourd, use the lino-cutting tool to engrave small eight-pointed stars (four lines crossing in the centre) all around the shell, piercing the centre of each star with the small gimlet. To decorate the darker green gourd, pierce the shell all around with the large gimlet.

LEFT: *Modern and minimal, the gourd on the left displays an effective yet simple pierced design. The clever technique of creating slits around the gourd in the centre means that a small amount of pressure applied to the top of the gourd will open the slits and allow the light to shine through. The combination of the engraving on the skin and piercing the centre of the stars on the gourd on the right makes a twinkling design.*

4 To display the gourds, insert a bunch of enclosed fairy lights from the same strand into the base of each one, plug in and turn on for a subtle, glimmering show.

maids in a row

This wonderful red cushion-shaped pumpkin is easy and rewarding to carve. It is one of the larger varieties and so lends itself to an adventurous, repetitive design. The well-known technique of folding and cutting paper to make a row of identical dolls has been adapted here to fit the front side of the pumpkin. A small amount of lino-cut decoration to suggest the costumes enhances the effect.

you will need

- large Rouge Vif d'Etampes pumpkin (or similar)
- water-soluble crayon
- craft knife
- kitchen knife
- pumpkin scoop
- lino-cutting tool
- ballpoint pen
- paper, for making a template
- small pointed scissors
- dressmakers' pins
- glass jar and nightlight or candle

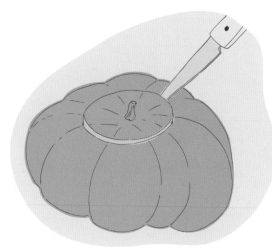

1 Mark a circle for the lid with the crayon and cut out with the craft knife (you may need to use the kitchen knife to release the flesh). Remove the 'lid'.

2 Scoop out the flesh with the special scoop, reducing the wall to no less than 1cm (½in). Rinse with water to remove all the debris.

3 Make a template by copying the drawing onto a piece of paper folded four times (this will give you five dolls), the size will depend on the size of your pumpkin. Make sure the outer edges of the skirt and the ends of the arms touch the folds, as these points will hold the template together. Cut out with scissors.

4 Open out the folded paper dolls and pin in place onto the surface of the pumpkin. Draw around the figures carefully with the ballpoint pen.

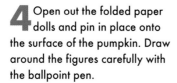

5 Remove the paper and begin to cut away all the areas between the dolls, making sure that the pen lines are also removed. You need to take care and work slowly as all the joints should be left uncut. Neaten up the inside edges of the flesh as you go.

tips

A squash or pumpkin usually has a better side, so inspect carefully before you begin to decorate, choosing the smoothest, blemish-free side to work on.

You can keep the pumpkin in the fridge until ready for use. It may also be revived after use by immersing in water until it rehydrates and regains its original firmness.

6 Using the lino-cutting tool, engrave the lines to indicate the apron, sleeves and hair of the dolls. Insert a large candle in a glass jar to illuminate the design.

BELOW: *You may like to carve a similar pumpkin with a row of dancing partners for the maids.*

autumn wreath

Pumpkins and squash come in miniature varieties and small sizes. Although dried gourds would make a longer-lasting wreath, these sweet dumpling squash and yellow squash work well when fixed to a sturdy twig wreath. If displayed outside during cold weather, they will last just as long as any other wreath made from living materials. The bright autumn leaves are shop-bought decorations, but you could easily collect your own – you will certainly achieve more variety in shape and colour with real leaves.

you will need

- 4 small sweet dumpling squash
- 4 small stripy yellow squash
- sturdy twig wreath base, at least 35cm (14in) in diameter
- craft knife
- florists' wire
- 8 decorative wired autumn leaves

1 Lay the wreath on a flat surface and position the different squash all around, balancing the shape, type and colour.

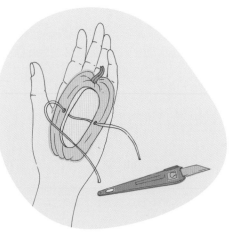

2 Using the craft knife, carefully cut away a small slice from the back of the squash so that it will sit snugly against the twigs on the wreath base. Insert the length of florists' wire through this cut-away section.

3 Place the squash onto the wreath and twist the wire firmly around the wreath to secure in place.

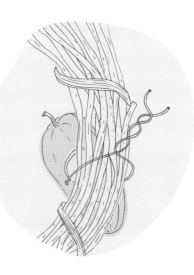

4 Continue attaching all the squash individually at equal intervals, cutting away a section at the back to ensure that they sit firmly before securing with the wire.

5 Push each leaf stem into the twig wreath between the squash and arrange by bending the wire down the centre. Secure behind by twisting the stem behind the end of the wires attaching the squash.

LEFT: *The rich tones of autumn leaves perfectly complement the cooler shades of the squash.*

garden lanterns

This gorgeous collection has been engraved with designs inspired by the garden. They are a mixed group of medium-sized pumpkins with soft flesh which is easier to extract, while the yellow one with the fern leaf design is, in fact, an unusual courgette with lovely smooth skin which is easy to decorate.

The images have been created by engraving the lines using a simple lino-cutting tool. This is very easy to do and when you become more adept, you will be able to draw with the tool without marking the design first.

1 Cut a circular hole in the top of the pumpkin using the craft knife (mark it first with the crayon if you are nervous about cutting a circle freehand). You may need to cut through again with a longer knife to release the 'lid'.

tip
Make sure that you cut the opening large enough to receive the glass jar containing the small candle.

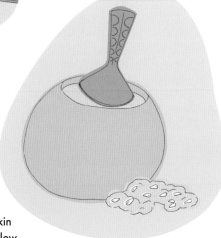

2 Pull out the flesh and seeds, then scoop out any remaining using the pumpkin scoop. As you reduce the thickness of the skin, use a smaller spoon and work around the inside to ensure an even thickness. You can rub it gently with the pot scourer to achieve a smooth finish. The skin needs to be only about 5mm (¼in) thick to allow light to glow through the lino-cut lines.

3 Use the crayon to mark the daisy motifs all around the pumpkin, spacing them evenly so they don't touch. If you are a confident artist, you may prefer to draw freehand as this produces a looser, more confident line.

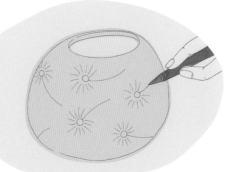

4 Using the lino-cutting tool and starting at the base of the stem, work the petals outwards from the centre of the flower. Continue until the surface of the pumpkin is decorated. Insert the glass jar and candle or nightlight.

RIGHT: *Each engraving is inspired by nature. From the left, the swirling tendrils are reminiscent of climbing plants, while the fern fronds are a reminder of spring when the fronds unfurl. The pretty floating flowers are inspired by the daisies in the lawn, and, as the pumpkin on the far right was being engraved, the leaves of the ash tree were falling all around.*

pierced gourd lanterns

At first glance, you may think these stylish lanterns have been expertly made from fine porcelain. In fact, they are ivory-coloured gourds that have been hollowed out and decorated with a simple pattern pierced through an even layer of skin. The economy of decoration is deliberate and doesn't interfere with or distract from the beautiful shape and colour.

The 'lids' have also been hollowed out and could be attached with fine wire to make a natural container – to do this, it is best to hollow out the gourd when it is 'cured' or thoroughly dry as there will inevitably be a little distortion if this is done when the gourd is freshly harvested.

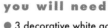

you will need

- 3 decorative white gourds
- craft knife
- water-soluble crayon
- small spoon with a long handle, for scooping
- flat-edged woodcarving tool
- bradawl, for marking holes
- small gimlet, for making holes
- candles and small glass jars

1 Using the craft knife, cut around the gourd to remove the 'lid'. If you don't feel confident cutting freehand, mark the line first with a water-soluble crayon. The opening should be just large enough to insert a small glass jar.

2 Remove the flesh and seeds with a spoon. If the gourd has just been picked, the flesh will be firm and you will need to ease or cut it away from the outer skin using the woodcarving tool. You will need to be patient and careful so that you end up with an even thickness of skin.

tip
It is a good idea to place the lanterns in a bowl of dry sand as this provides a secure base, allowing you to adjust the position. Use a candle in a glass jar and make sure the flame is beneath the opening, otherwise the heat will distort the shape.

3 Use the bradawl to prick the skin carefully around the edge of the rim and in three wavy rows around the body of the hollowed-out gourd. This is your guide for piercing the holes.

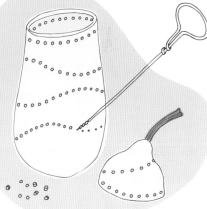

LEFT: *The pale colours, distinctive shapes and subtle decoration of these beautiful gourds mean they could be mistaken for contemporary porcelain.*

4 Use the gimlet to pierce the skin following the pricked lines. Small bits of debris will probably fall inside the gourd and can be brushed out later. Pierce the lid in the same way. Insert the glass jar containing the candle.

monogrammed field pumpkin

The field pumpkin is the most common variety and the most readily available from markets, farms and grocery stores alike. The advantages are its symmetrical shape and the softness of the flesh, making it very easy for children to carve.

There is so much more to do with this luminous orange pumpkin than carving scary Halloween masks, and this engaging project shows you how to create your own monogram. It would make the most inspired and elegant gift for a friend who celebrates a birthday in the autumn.

you will need
- large field pumpkin
- craft knife
- kitchen knife
- assorted scooping spoons and special pumpkin scoop
- paper and pen, for making a template
- dressmakers' pins
- water-soluble crayon (if you want to draw freehand)
- large gimlet
- lino-cutting tool
- glass jar and slow-burning candle or nightlight

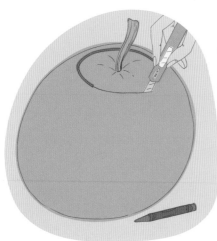

1 Mark a circle at the top of the pumpkin – it needs to be large enough for you to reach in with your hand. Cut out with the craft knife (this makes a neater line), then make a deeper cut along the lines using the kitchen knife, to allow you to remove the lid.

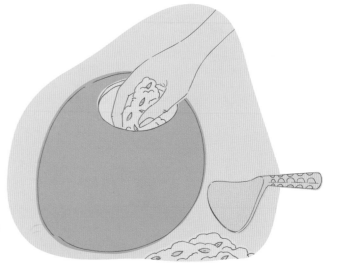

2 Pull out the flesh and the seeds, first using your hand, then using the scoops and spoons to remove the remaining flesh. The special pumpkin scoop is ideal to use on a large variety like this, as it has a flattened side which removes the flesh most efficiently. The shell needs to be about 8mm (⅜in) thick. This is really only important on the front of the pumpkin where the design will be carved.

tips

If you can draw your design freehand without the use of the template, you will create a freer, more flowing image. The ultimate aim is to learn to 'draw' the pattern directly with the knife.

After a while, your pumpkin may dry out and bend a little, especially from the heat of a candle. To revive, immerse in a bucket of water for half an hour and it will rehydrate and become firm again. Store in a cool place to prolong its life.

LEFT: *This softly glowing, beautifully engraved field pumpkin would make an elegant centrepiece at an autumn party.*

3 Make a paper template of your chosen initial by copying from a newspaper or magazine, or by printing a large-scale initial from a computer (most computers offer a range of typefaces and sizes). Add the leafy garland around the initial. Pin evenly to the front of the pumpkin and mark the design by pricking with a pin all along the lines. Remove the template and your design is ready for carving. If you are more confident, draw your design directly onto the pumpkin using the crayon.

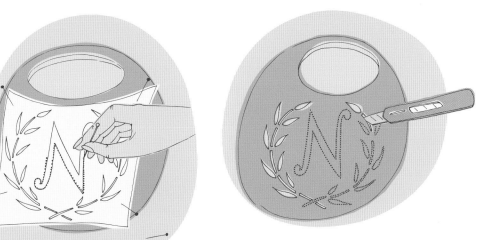

4 Use the craft knife to cut out the leaves and stems of the garland. Make sure you do not connect the leaves or the stem, or the pumpkin will be less stable. As you cut, carefully push the pieces inside the pumpkin for removal later.

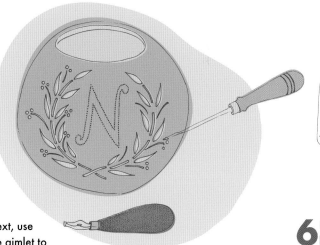

5 Next, use the gimlet to create the 'berries' around the garland. Using the lino-cutting tool, engrave the stems and around the line of the initial.

6 Finally, cut out the letter shape in the centre of the design. Turn the pumpkin over and shake out the debris. Insert a glass jar containing a nightlight or candle.

tulip gourds

Gourds are usually inedible, purely decorative examples from the large family of cucurbits, pumpkins, squash and gourds, and are characterized by a dense, woody skin. There is a wide variety of endlessly fascinating colours, sizes and shapes. When left to dry, the skin becomes harder and the flesh shrivels inside, meaning that they will last indefinitely in a dry atmosphere. Due to these qualities, gourds lend themselves to small lanterns – here they have been hollowed out and cleverly turned into tulip flowers with a green wire stem. When using these highly decorative gourds, it is best only to add minimal decoration.

you will need

- selection of small decorative gourds
- craft knife
- small scooping spoon
- woodcarving tool
- nylon pot scourer
- water-soluble crayon
- medium gimlet
- small gimlet
- green plastic-coated gardening wire, 2mm (⅛in) thick
- nightlights

1 Slice the top from the yellow gourd. Discard the lid and begin to remove the flesh and seeds (a fully ripe gourd will only contain dried and shrivelled matter which will be easier to remove). Use a teaspoon to remove the flesh gradually. As you need to remove it all and leave just the hard outer skin, it is helpful to use a woodcarving tool to prize the flesh away before you spoon it out.

tip

To create a 'mixed bunch' of tulips, decorate each gourd in a different way, following the individual shape and pattern of each one.

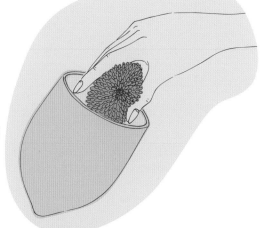

2 Rub the pot scourer around the inside to remove any remaining flesh and to smooth the inside.

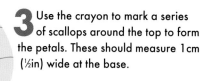

3 Use the crayon to mark a series of scallops around the top to form the petals. These should measure 1cm (½in) wide at the base.

4 Use the craft knife to cut away the skin around the marked petals.

5 Draw a crayon guideline around the gourd about 1cm (½in) below the base of each petal and use the medium gimlet to make a series of holes around this line, spacing them 5mm (¼in) apart. Rub away the crayon line.

6 Make a hole through the base of the tulip with the small gimlet. Cut a 30cm (12in) length of gardening wire, twist one end into a spiral and thread the other end through the hole you have made. If the wire feels a little loose, make another couple of twists in the wire on the outside. Insert a nightlight into each flower and display by pushing into the soil packed into a large flowerpot.

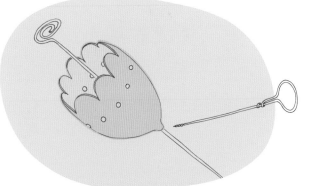

lino-cut squash

Some squash or pumpkins are very dense and grow into such interesting shapes that it is difficult to hollow them out to turn into lanterns. You can, however, decorate them simply in a way that enhances and exaggerates the natural form. Why not do this and display them for a couple of days in a large bowl before you cut them up and use them to create a delicious meal?

If you do this, don't peel the squash first. Simply cut into pieces, each with a part of the decoration on the skin, bake in the oven and surprise your guests when they discover a uniquely patterned vegetable on their plate.

you will need

● small, hard squash, such as acorn or butternut
● lino-cutting tool

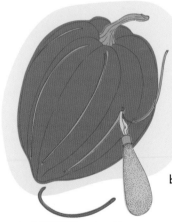

1 An acorn squash has ridges and furrows which are usually fairly evenly spaced, running from the base to the stem. Use the lino-cutting tool to cut a line along the base of each of the furrows, leaving a gap at both ends.

2 Make smaller cuts radiating out from these lines, creating a feathered effect. These should run towards the stem. Start each one from the central vertical line working outwards – this helps to create a tapered end.

3 A butternut squash has a smooth skin and is slightly pear shaped. Use the lino-cutting tool to create two horizontal lines around the base of the elongated section.

4 On the upper half, create a series of vertical lines ending just below the stem. On the more bulbous base section, create several spirals to fill the lower section. This is easy to do as long as you turn the squash rather than the lino-cutting tool to create an even line.

LEFT AND RIGHT: *Butternut squash have wonderful smooth skins and are a lovely buff colour. As well as being delicious to eat (especially when baked), they are a beautiful form to decorate and you will be inspired to create your own designs.*

little gem nightlights

These small, round, green pumpkins are called Little Gem or Rolets and are most usually baked whole in the oven, with butter, salt and pepper added through a small opening at the top. Alternatively, they make excellent little nightlight holders, with the hollowed-out interior glowing yellow when illuminated.

It is very easy to make patterns by using a lino-cutting tool to remove part of the skin to reveal the yellow flesh. As they are so small and therefore quick to make, why not make them for an autumn dinner party and give each guest their own lantern as part of the place setting.

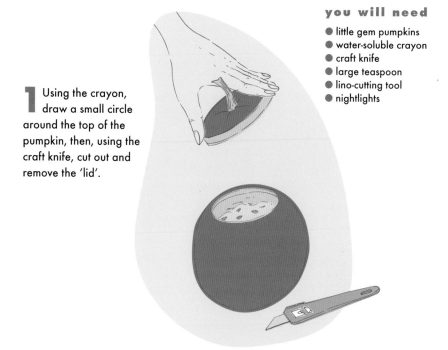

1 Using the crayon, draw a small circle around the top of the pumpkin, then, using the craft knife, cut out and remove the 'lid'.

you will need
● little gem pumpkins
● water-soluble crayon
● craft knife
● large teaspoon
● lino-cutting tool
● nightlights

2 Use the teaspoon to scoop out the flesh and seeds. Try to make the walls even and no thicker than about 4mm (³⁄₁₆in).

3 Starting in the middle of one side, begin to cut a spiral with the lino-cutting tool. Hold the tool firmly to create an even line. Remember to cut away from yourself – it helps to turn the pumpkin rather than the blade of the tool. Finish the spiral, leaving 5mm (¼in) undecorated at the top and base.

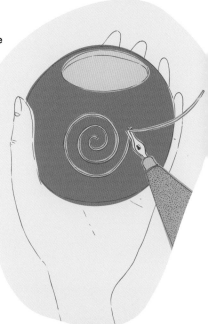

4 Turn the pumpkin so that you can engrave a spiral on the opposite side, leaving the same margins. Now repeat the spirals, one between each one already cut. Finish with small V shapes between the spirals at the top edge. Place a nightlight inside.

BELOW AND BELOW LEFT: *Use your imagination to carve different patterns on each pumpkin. If using as a place setting, you could carve each with the guest's initial.*

sweet dumpling candle holders

The brilliant colour of the sweet dumpling squash, as well as its rather upholstered cushion-like shape, makes it an ideal candle holder as it sits so well on the base. This couldn't be a simpler project and, when the candles have burnt down, you can remove the stub and use the deliciously flavoured squash to bake, use as a pie filling or turn into soup.

Select the height and colour of your candles carefully – the interesting wax tones of pink, orange and green chosen here beautifully complement the rich yellow skin which is splashed with a deep ochre along the crevices.

you will need

- assortment of 3 sweet dumpling squash
- 3 short candles in green, pink and orange
- ballpoint pen
- craft knife

1 Remove the stalk from the top of the squash and place the candle in the dip remaining. Draw around the base with the ballpoint pen and remove the candle.

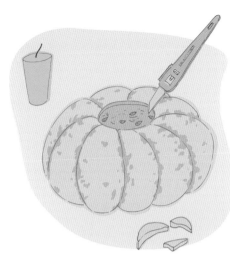

2 Using the craft knife, cut around the marked line, pulling out the small pieces of squash as you go. Try fitting the candle in place and cut more squash away if necessary, always ensuring that the candle fits tightly in the hole.

tip

If you want to cook and eat the squash when the candle has burnt down, when you remove the candle stub make sure that there is no wax or debris remaining in the hole.

house in the woods

This lovely Hansel and Gretel house design sits in a spooky wood – you can almost imagine a witch creeping around in the rooms behind the windows! The image has been drawn directly onto the watermelon skin – as with the Curious Cats project on page 74, you can rub away any marks until you are happy with your design. Or if you wish, make a paper template from the illustration shown here and transfer the image by the pin method shown on page 43.

This project is suitable for any large, soft-fleshed pumpkin. A very ripe watermelon has been used here, the skin being a lovely yellowy green colour. The advantage of using a watermelon is that you can eat the delicious flesh as you carve it out – try making a fruit salad with watermelon and strawberries.

1 Draw around the top of the melon and use the craft knife and kitchen knife to cut out and remove the 'lid'. Put the 'lid' to one side. Pull out the seeds and remove the flesh with a combination of spoon and scoop. The wall should be smooth and about 1cm (½in) thick.

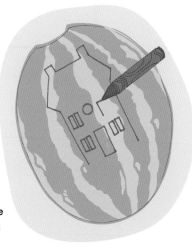

2 Hold the best side of the melon towards you and, using the photo as a guide, draw your version of the house in crayon on the top two-thirds of the melon.

3 Draw the trees, each with four branches, on each side of the house, making sure that most of the branches connect to the house or to the edge of your design.

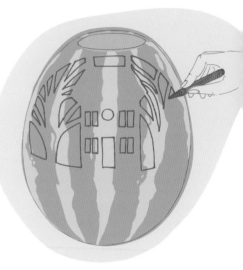

LEFT: *This detailed fairy-tale house would look delightful sitting alongside the maids-in-a-row pumpkin featured on page 24.*

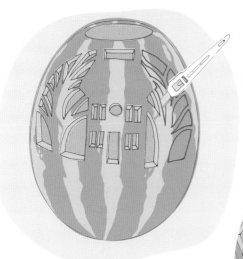

4 Use the craft knife to cut out the main windows (each with two panes), the door, the circular window above the door, the space above the chimney and, finally, between all the branches of the trees.

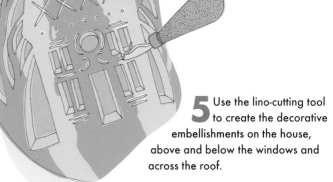

5 Use the lino-cutting tool to create the decorative embellishments on the house, above and below the windows and across the roof.

6 Use the lino-cutting tool to outline the house and chimney and to create a garden path from the front door. Engrave tufts of grass on each side of the path. Engrave a line to act as a frame around the decorated opening. Insert the glass jar and candle.

snow crystal

The beautiful pale skin of the unusual cotton candy pumpkin lends itself to this pretty repeated snowflake design. When the pumpkin is lit at dusk, it gives off an ethereal wintry glow. The pale flesh is revealed by using a lino-cutting tool to make a simple star of four crossed lines which have been embellished to create a stylized snowflake. If you have a good eye and a steady hand, you don't really need to mark the design first – just use the tool to make a freehand drawing.

you will need

- cotton candy pumpkin
- craft knife
- kitchen knife
- assorted scoops and spoons
- nylon pot scourer
- water-soluble crayon (optional)
- lino-cutting tool
- glass jar and nightlight or candle

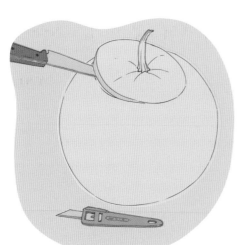

1 Mark a circle around the stem at the top of the pumpkin large enough to insert your hand. Cut through the flesh with the craft knife along this line and remove the lid. If the flesh is particularly thick you may need to use a sharp kitchen knife to make a deeper cut.

2 Pull out as much of the seeds and flesh as you can with your hands and then begin to scoop out the remainder using a spoon or scoop. You need to make the shell about 8mm (⅜in) thick and this should be even all around. Be careful not to scoop away too much flesh in one part.

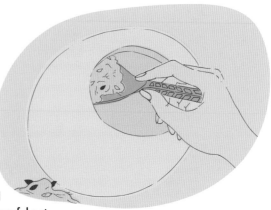

3 Shake out all the debris from the inside of the pumpkin and insert the pot scourer. Rub evenly around the inside of the shell to create a uniform and smooth finish. This will enhance the design when the pumpkin is lit as the light will shine through as an even glow.

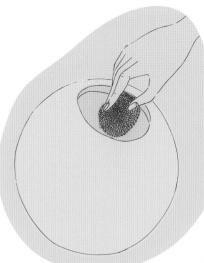

4 If you need reassurance, mark the position of the snowflakes evenly around the pumpkin using the crayon. If you prefer to 'draw' freehand, use the lino-cutting tool to make two lines crossed at right angles. The length of these lines will in some part depend on the size of the pumpkin that you are decorating, but they should be about 4cm (1½in) long.

5 Now intersect these lines with two more lines, creating a star. You may find it easier to work from the centre outwards, so that the lines are tapered at the outer ends.

6 Just before the end of each line, cut two new short lines at an angle of 45 degrees to the main lines. This creates the snowflake effect. Finally, insert the glass jar and nightlight or candle.

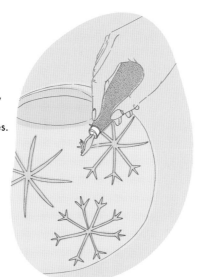

BELOW: *This simple yet effective design would work well on any pale-skinned pumpkin, gourd or squash.*

bird feeders

It is so important to feed native birds during winter when their normal food is scarce. Small pumpkins or squash make wonderful containers that can be fashioned into practical bird feeders, and a variety of garden birds will enjoy pecking at the bright orange flesh as well as the seeds contained inside.

These colourful, easy-to-make examples are a great project for children. Long hangers, made from green garden wire, mean that the feeders will be less accessible to cats. The use of coloured bottle tops at the base of the squash and at the hanging end stops the wire slicing through the squash.

you will need

- 3 contrasting small squash or pumpkins (such as rolet, sweet dumpling, touch of autumn)
- water-soluble crayon
- kitchen knife
- scooping spoon
- bradawl
- yellow and red plastic bottle tops (2 required for each squash)
- 1m (1 yard) of green plastic-coated garden wire, 1.5mm (¹⁄₁₆in) thick
- wirecutters
- pliers
- wild bird seed or fruit suet treat

1 Draw a circle around the squash about one-third of the way down from the top. Slice off the top using a sharp kitchen knife.

2 Scoop out the flesh with a spoon, leaving the walls approximately 2cm (¾in) thick.

3 Using the bradawl, make two holes approximately 1cm (½in) apart in the yellow bottle lid. Repeat with the red lid.

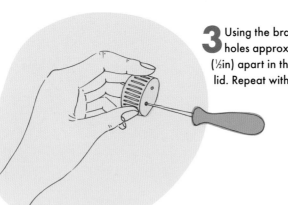

4 Fold the wire in half and thread both ends through the top of the yellow bottle lid.

5 Make two corresponding holes at the base of the squash and push the two ends of the wire through from beneath. Pull firmly so that the bottle top is tight against the base. Thread the two ends of the wire through the top of the red bottle lid, twist the wire together using the pliers, bend over the end and cover inside the lid.

6 Fill the upturned squash with bird seed or fruit suet treat, then hang the bird feeder from a suitable tree branch.

tips

The squash or pumpkins will last for several days outside, especially if the weather is cool (but not extremely cold). If it begins to decompose, simply replace with a new one on the existing wire.

If you make a group of bird feeders, try using a selection of feeds, either seeds, nuts or suet mixtures – each one will attract a different species of bird.

ABOVE: *The bottle-top which forms the hanging loop.*
BELOW AND RIGHT: *These feeders are a great way of introducing wildlife into your garden.*

rose window

This decorative cut-out design was inspired by intricate rose windows often seen in churches and cathedrals. A circle has been cut out from the top of the squash and, when all the flesh has been scooped out, the squash has been turned upside down, working the design on what would have been the base.

Like the Crown Prince squash seen in the daisy bud lantern project on page 90, this deeply contoured, slightly knobbly squash has very hard flesh and it will take time to carve it away. To turn it into a lantern, just place the squash over one or more small lighted candles, and the cut-through decoration will allow plenty of space for the heat to escape.

you will need

- large green-orange knobbly squash, such as Marina di Chioggia
- water-soluble crayon
- craft knife
- kitchen knife
- woodcarving tool
- pumpkin scoop and assorted spoons
- gimlet
- glass jar and slow-burning candle

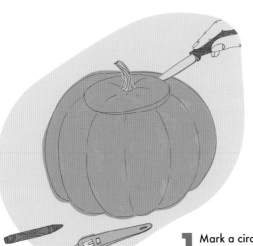

1 Mark a circle on the top of the squash at least 10cm (4in) in diameter. Cut through with a craft knife and use the sharp kitchen knife to deepen the cut in order to release the 'lid'.

2 Pull out the seeds with your hand and begin to chip out the flesh. You will need to use the woodcarving tool as well as cross-hatching the flesh with the tip of the kitchen knife. Remove the shredded bits with the scoop or spoon. Be patient as this will take some time. The wall needs to be 1.5cm (⅝in) thick.

3 Turn the squash over and, using crayon, start to draw your design on the base of the squash. Begin with eight petal shapes set around the central boss, leaving a gap of about 5mm (¼in) in between.

4 Carefully cut these petals out using the craft knife, leaving the gap between the cut lines. Take care not to cut away the centre.

5 Below each petal draw another two petals, then cut out carefully, leaving an uncut margin between.

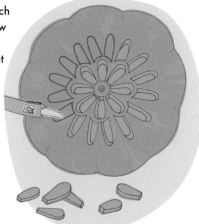

6 Finally, use the gimlet to make a circle of holes between the top edges of these outer petals. Place the carved pumpkin over a glass jar containing a slow-burning candle.

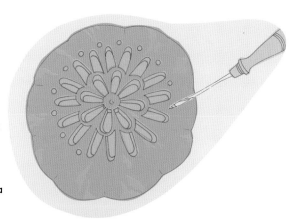

tip
You could also light this lantern with a torch or fairy lights.

BELOW: *The strong, clean cut-away shapes make a striking lantern, created here with a Marina di Chioggia pumpkin.*

curious cats

Cats are universally popular, and they seem to inhabit a friendly domestic world as well as a world of mystery and magic. Their simple, symmetrical faces with staring eyes make them the perfect image for a small pumpkin lantern designed to glow in the dark. Along with the carved face on page 86, this is another project perfect for Halloween.

All the decoration here is made with the lino-cutting tool, which engraves the surface. As the flesh has been removed and the wall thinned substantially, the light will penetrate these engraved lines. To create a dramatic effect, the only areas cut through entirely are the slits in the cats' eyes. Any small, soft-fleshed pumpkin can be used for this project.

you will need

- small field pumpkins or similar
- water-soluble crayon
- craft knife
- kitchen knife
- pumpkin scoop or small spoon
- lino-cutting tool
- small glass jars and slow-burning candles

1 Using crayon, draw a circle at the top of your pumpkin just large enough for you to able to remove all the flesh and seeds. Cut along this line with the craft knife. If necessary, insert the kitchen knife to help detach the 'lid'. Scoop out the insides, reducing the wall of the pumpkin to a thickness of approximately 8mm (⅜in).

2 Draw a cat's face onto the front of the pumpkin in crayon, using the illustration as a guide. You can wipe away the crayon lines and redraw them until you are satisfied with the face.

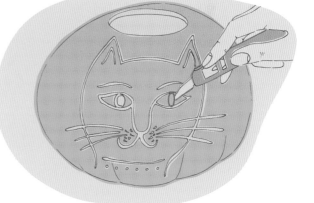

3 Cut away the drawn lines with the lino-cutting tool – begin with the outline, then work on the nose, eyes, mouth and whiskers. Add the collar and cut away small nicks at the base of the whiskers.

4 Finally, use the craft knife to cut right through the slits in the centre of each eye. Insert a small candle in a jar to illuminate.

LEFT: *This friendly feline brings a touch of fun to the garden when displayed on an old gate post.*

fairy light cut-outs

The firm flesh and manageable size of the Kabocha squash and its cousin, the Kuri, make them ideal squash for these inverted lanterns. Like the Rose Window on page 70, the design is also cut through at the top, allowing the heat from a candle to escape. For a more durable and charming way of lighting the lantern, why not use a string of fairy lights, inserting a few together into the base of each squash. This has the added advantage that the remaining lights can be arranged around the lanterns, making a pretty display.

Like the Rose Window on page 70

you will need

- 2 squash – one green Kabocha and one orange Kuri
- craft knife
- kitchen knife
- woodcarving tool
- assorted spoons and scoops
- water-soluble crayon
- string of outdoor fairy lights

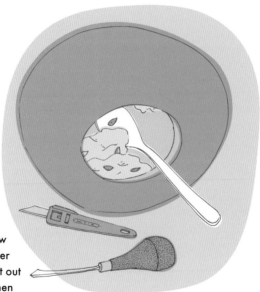

1 Turn the squash over and draw a circle 8cm (3¼in) in diameter around the centre of the base. Cut out with the craft knife, using the kitchen knife to release if necessary. Use a combination of the woodcarving tool, knife, spoon and scoop to release the very hard flesh. Reduce the wall to 1cm (½in) thick.

tip

Be patient and careful when removing the flesh from the hard squash. A woodcarving tool helps to chip away the flesh. These are some of the most delicious squash so save the flesh to make an appetizing soup.

2 Turn the squash over and draw a circle around the stem at the top. Draw four similar-sized circles equidistantly around the sides.

LEFT: Fairy lights are such a pretty way to illuminate these carved squash. Sometimes the simplest designs can be the most effective.

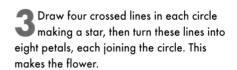

3 Draw four crossed lines in each circle making a star, then turn these lines into eight petals, each joining the circle. This makes the flower.

4 Use the craft knife to cut out all the spaces between the petals, making sure that each petal is attached to the edge of the circle (otherwise the flower will fall out). Rub away the crayon guidelines. To finish, cut a small circle in the centre of each flower and insert the fairy lights. Trim the stalk so that it is flush with the skin. Insert the fairy lights and switch on.

fig leaf gourd

This unusual, large fig leaf gourd has a lovely green speckled skin which resembles a watermelon, although it is surprisingly tough. This means that it is necessary to use a special small saw to cut away any of the hollowed out shell – this is not difficult but you will need to first drill a small hole in which to insert the saw before you start. The flesh is white, edible and rather unremarkable in flavour. Unlike other squash or pumpkins, the high water content of the flesh means it lends itself well to preserving in a sugar syrup.

you will need
- fig leaf gourd
- water-soluble crayon
- small gimlet
- special pumpkin saw
- small pointed kitchen knife
- assorted spoons and scoops
- nylon pot scourer
- large gimlet
- craft knife
- small glass jar and nightlight or candle

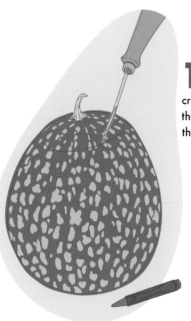

1 Mark a circle around the stem at the top of the gourd with the crayon, then drill a small hole with the small gimlet at one point along this line.

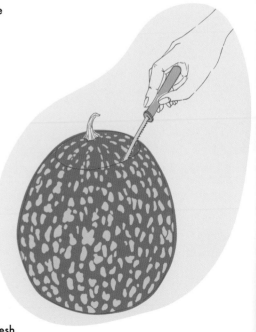

2 Insert the pumpkin saw and carefully saw along the line that you have drawn. When you have sawn all around the circle, pull on the stem to release the lid. If it doesn't come away easily, you may have to insert a sharp kitchen knife to cut through the thickness of flesh.

3 Pull out as much flesh and seeds as you can with your hand. To remove the remaining flesh, use an assortment of spoons and scoops. The special pumpkin scoop works well on this gourd. Try to make the inner base as flat as possible – rubbing the inside with the pot scourer helps you to attain an even thickness of 8mm (⅜in). Rinse out the interior with water.

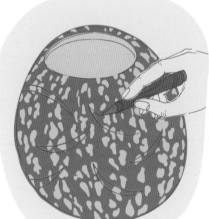

4 Pat the skin dry and, using the crayon, draw simple willow-shaped leaves evenly spaced all around the gourd. Try to create a free-flowing effect, almost as if the leaves are falling in autumn.

5 Use the small gimlet to drill a hole at one end of each of the leaves, as you did with the lid, then insert the saw and gently but firmly saw around the leaf shape until it falls away. Repeat until all the leaves are completed.

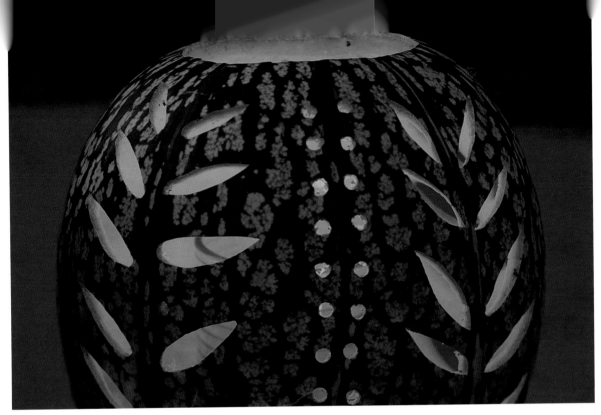

ABOVE: *This similar sized gourd has been decorated with vertical ash leaves alternated with a double row of pierced holes. As the skin is so hard, restrict your design to simple shapes that are easier to remove.*

6 Use the large gimlet to drill holes in between the cut-away leaves, and the small gimlet to make a circle of smaller holes around the larger hole. Shake out the debris from inside the gourd and trim any rough edges in the flesh around the leaves with the craft knife. To light, insert a candle or nightlight in a glass jar and place inside the gourd.

halloween face

Here is the perfect project for a Halloween party, and it's ideal for young children to make. Carving the large orange field pumpkins is a Halloween tradition, but in reality many of these are crude and unimaginative, so here is the opportunity to make something more individual and memorable. The simple techniques of cutting away and engraving create different lighting effects – the light pierces, glows, glimmers and sparkles.

you will need

- large, smooth-skinned field pumpkin
- water-soluble crayon
- craft knife
- kitchen knife
- assorted scooping spoons, including special pumpkin scoop
- large gimlet
- paper and pen
- dressmaker's pins
- sharp bradawl
- lino-cutting tool
- flat-edged woodcarving tool
- glass jar and large, squat, slow-burning candle

1 Mark a crayon circle at the top of the pumpkin, large enough to insert your hand. Cut out first with the craft knife (to make a neat line), then cut deeper with the kitchen knife to cut away. You can pierce the lid with the gimlet to make air holes if you want to use it when the pumpkin is alight.

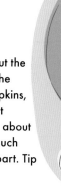

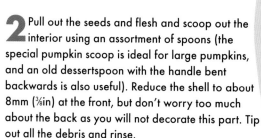

2 Pull out the seeds and flesh and scoop out the interior using an assortment of spoons (the special pumpkin scoop is ideal for large pumpkins, and an old dessertspoon with the handle bent backwards is also useful). Reduce the shell to about 8mm (⅜in) at the front, but don't worry too much about the back as you will not decorate this part. Tip out all the debris and rinse.

3 Draw your face design onto a sheet of paper that fits the front of your pumpkin. Fix in place with dressmakers' pins and prick out the design through the paper onto the skin using the bradawl. Remove the paper.

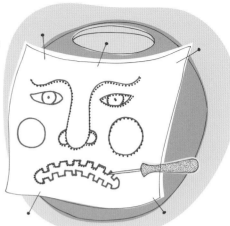

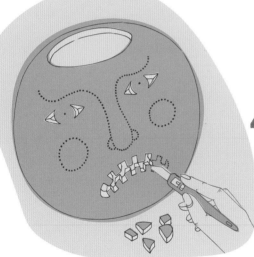

4 Refer to your paper template as you begin to carve your design. Carefully cut out the whites of the eyes with the craft knife, taking care to leave the pupil intact. In the same way, cut out the spaces between the teeth.

5 Use the lino-cutting tool to engrave the lines around the eyes, eyebrows and mouth. Make a circle on each cheek and use the woodcarving tool to remove the outer skin,. Do the same on the two nostrils.

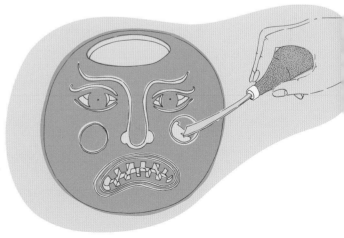

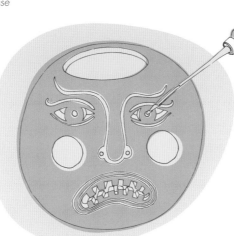

ABOVE: *Place the glowing lantern in a front window of your darkened house and keep evil spirits at bay!*

6 Use the gimlet to carefully drill the hole for the iris in the centre of the eyes. In the same way, make a hole for the nostrils. Insert the glass jar and candle. When lit, you can replace the lid if you wish.

tip
To revive the pumpkin, immerse it in water and keep cool (the fridge is ideal) when not lit. It will last for a number of days if looked after in this way.

daisy bud lantern

The Crown Prince squash is one of the most beautiful of all the varieties due to its silky, patinated blue-grey skin. Its deep orange flesh, which tastes of sweet chestnuts, is delicious and versatile.

When it comes to decorating or carving, you will need some strength and patience. The flesh is very hard and difficult to scoop out, and you will need to use more than just a spoon – a flat-ended woodcarving tool helps, as well as cross-hatching the flesh with the tip of a knife to break it into shreds which are easier to remove. It is well worth the effort, but keep your design simple and try to enhance the exquisite qualities of the squash itself. When lit, this simple design allows the squash to glow from the decorated opening, with a little light shining through the engraved lines.

you will need
- medium-large Crown Prince squash
- ballpoint pen
- craft knife
- pointed kitchen knife with a long blade
- flat-ended woodcarving tool
- pumpkin scoop
- lino-cutting tool
- candle and glass jar

1 Draw a circle around the stem at the top of the squash and cut out with the craft knife. You may need to insert a kitchen knife with a longer blade to reach through the thick flesh.

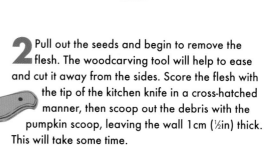

2 Pull out the seeds and begin to remove the flesh. The woodcarving tool will help to ease and cut it away from the sides. Score the flesh with the tip of the kitchen knife in a cross-hatched manner, then scoop out the debris with the pumpkin scoop, leaving the wall 1cm (½in) thick. This will take some time.

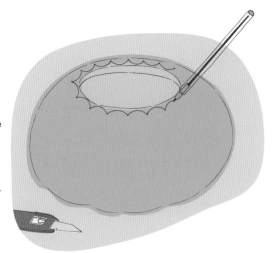

3 Use the ballpoint pen to draw a series of scallops around the opening, the rounded edge facing inwards. Use the craft knife to cut them out carefully outside the pen line, revealing the decorated edge.

4 Using the lino-cutting tool, create a line radiating down from each scallop all around the body of the squash. Repeat at each point so that you end up with a shape that looks like an opening daisy bud. Neaten off any thick flesh around the opening. Place a candle inside a glass jar and place inside the squash.

RIGHT: *The welcoming glow radiating from this pumpkin makes it perfect for lighting entrances and pathways.*

useful contacts

Most large supermarkets and grocery stores sell special pumpkin carving kits at Halloween, alongside mountains of orange field pumpkins. Pumpkins, squash and gourds can be found, when in season, at all good supermarket chains, farm stores, farmers' markets, and wholefood stores. In addition, the websites listed on the right provide helpful information.

Pumpkin carving kits

www.pumpkinmasters.com
www.yankeeharvest.com

Seeds and information on growing pumpkins

www.organiccatalogue.com
www.backyardgardener.com

Suppliers

www.localharvest.org

index

acknowledgements

Very many thanks to Michael Rand, our inventive allotment neighbour, for allowing us to photograph some of the pumpkins on his lovely plot. Thanks also to other plot-holders at Fitzroy Park allotments for providing marvellous props and backgrounds.

I want to thank Gillian Haslam, my editor, for making the book run so smoothly, Christine Wood for her simple, good design, and Trina Dalziel for creating such lovely illustrations.

My gratitude extends, of course, to my husband, Heini Schneebeli, for his beautiful photographs. I am also very grateful to Tamasin Cole for her practical help and generous advice.

Apart from those grown by myself, the pumpkins featured in this book mainly come from Mr C R Upton of Slinfold, Sussex, who is an inspiration to all pumpkin growers and pumpkin admirers.

Lastly, I would like to thank my publisher Cindy Richards, who is always alert to good ideas.